AL NESTLER'S SOUTHWEST

COTTONWOOD WASH — *Oil*, 18 x 24 inches

The rugged and beautiful Southwe.

AL NESTLER'S SOUTHWEST

interpreted by one of Arizona's foremost painters

With a preface by Robert MacLeod

NORTHLAND PRESS, FLAGSTAFF, ARIZONA · NINETEEN SEVENTY

THIS EDITION IS LIMITED TO 1500 COPIES

LIBRARY OF CONGRESS CATALOG CARD NUMBER: 70–121017
SBN 87358–052–4

DEDICATED TO LOREN, RONALD, AND NORMAN

CONTENTS

LIST OF ILLUSTRATIONS

PREFACE

AL NESTLER'S SOUTHWEST — Arizona, Colorado, Utah, New Mexico, California, and a corner of Old Mexico — as shared with us here, is uniquely Al Nestler's, and now yours and mine as well: forty years of it, presented through the perceptive eye and skilled hand of a fine landscape painter.

In forty years, a man can cover a great deal of ground and hundreds of square yards of canvas and paper. Here we have the distillation of all those years and miles and hundreds of paintings and drawings.

Al Nestler's orbit has at times swung far afield from the corner of his world offered here, reaching out to the length and breadth of Old Mexico, Spain and Portugal, source and prototype of their lineal descendant, the American Southwest, to which his deep interest has always swung back, regenerated, reinforced, and augmented.

Southwesterners know their landscape — the seductive and deceptive softness of rounded hills and pine-clad mountain slopes, the harsh red rocks, the anything-but-barren desert, the awesome canyons, the forbidding, icy peaks, the wonderful thousand-year-old structures of the Anasazi and Hohokam, the ever-changing mood and color. Now to see all this interpreted by Al Nestler with brush and felt pen, with oil and water, and pigment and ink, is to learn that we have never really seen it before; here is a revelation of shapes, designs, compositions, a richness of color, an interplay of line and mass and mood which we have missed, for all our awareness of how moving and beautiful it all is. Mr. Nestler sees better and deeper and truer than we do and shows us, not to impress with how penetrating is his vision, but to say, "See what is really there!"

I believe Al achieves this largely by stripping away the non-essentials of minute detail and minor elements of landscape which tend to distract the eye from the big pattern, the basic design and rhythm — and by showing us the underlying structure, the dominant mood.

All this is done with a surprisingly simple palette;

specifically, Cadmium Yellow light, Cadmium Orange, Cadmium Red light, Alizarin Crimson, Cobalt Blue, Ultramarine Blue, Thalo Green, and White — with two exceptions, only primary colors. It takes a thorough understanding of the laws of color and light to be able to achieve the color and value required without resorting to the endless array of fancifully named tints and shades.

Mr. Nestler also knows that a good painting can only be produced on a foundation of the essential building blocks — drawing, composition, design, color, and dark and light values — and that if any of these is faulty or lacking, the whole structure will collapse. This is what he teaches his students, what he looks for when he accepts a painting for display in La Galeria, his gallery in Sedona, Arizona, and what he uses with such success in his own work.

The one ingredient I find lacking in AL NESTLER'S SOUTHWEST is an intangible which could not be included: an indication of the respect for his great ability on the part of professionals and amateurs and those who own his paintings, and the warm affection for the man himself on the part of those of us who are privileged to know him.

ROBERT MACLEOD

Since the above was written, before this book went to press, Al Nestler died in his sleep, 29 May 1970. Earlier that week he had made the last two drawings for this book. As with all great painters, none can fill his place; similarly, for his friends who loved him, there can be no substitute.

R. M.

INTRODUCTION

THE OLD AND THE ANCIENT THINGS, the history and the ruins of long ago, Indians and artifacts, books of travel and adventure—these were the things I found I needed even as a youngster. I think I have always had a great affinity and yearning for the wide-open spaces, the faraway places. At eight or nine I was one of the neighborhood Robin Hood's band. He was our hero and we even had suits of Lincoln green made for us by our mothers. Then came years of Boy Scouting, as a Scout, a Scoutmaster, and finally as Assistant Scout Executive at St. Joseph, Missouri. About this time I considered going into the United States Forest Service but studies at the St. Joseph Art School under Rupert Hamilton started me on an exciting career in which I could combine my love for the wild places and the beauty of the landscapes by portraying them in pencil, paints and canvases.

On my first trip West I was on the Burlington railroad from St. Joseph to Denver when I remembered reading that the great peaks of the Continental Divide could be seen from more than a hundred miles away. With my face glued to the window, about midmorning after topping a long grade in Nebraska, sure enough there they were, those great shining mountains, the backbone of the continent, glistening in the morning sun. I threw open the window and promptly had both eyes filled with cinders from that coal-burning engine.

Enos Mills, writer and naturalist, was owner of Longs Peak Inn when I wrote to apply for a job. For several summers I worked there in this magnificent area at the foot of Longs Peak. With considerable time to myself, I filled many sketch books with drawings, watercolors, and small oils which I placed in the Inn's gift shop for sale. These sales to tourists kept me in paints and supplies.

Then I worked for the Pikes Peak Ocean-to-Ocean Highway Association with headquarters in St. Joseph, Missouri. Travel and the far places lured me. I was married now and we traveled in a special-built Dodge with the map of the Highway painted

1

on the sides. Fortunately when our advertising work in a community was finished, I had time to sketch and paint. While traveling through Nevada, Utah, and Colorado there were hours to do a number of small oils.

When we reached Columbus, Ohio, our paychecks failed to arrive as the area manager, Mr. Judson, was on his way to California. Completely broke, I walked into an artists' supply store which had an attractive art gallery. With about fifteen small canvases of far western mountains and canyons under my arm, I asked the gentleman in charge whether he would be interested in seeing my work. In a somewhat less than enthusiastic tone he replied that he doubted he could use any, but would look. The little paintings were a gay splashy lot as I placed them in a long row on the counter — snowy peaks, redwalled canyons, tumbly clouds over the desert. He studied them for a long time, asked many questions about where they were painted and where I had studied. Finally he discussed the paintings with a woman from the gallery. "How much do you want for them?" I told him I had no idea of the selling price for art in Ohio. "Would you take $25.00 each for the group?" My knees buckled and my jaws snapped as I shakily replied, "I think that would be a fair enough price." This sale remains my record to this day for the amount of paintings sold at one time. I would have taken $25.00 for the entire group under the circumstances. During the years to come this gallery sold many of my paintings.

After the Ocean-to-Ocean Highway Association folded when the government took over the designating and marking of all highways, the call of the West took us to Grand Junction, Colorado, where we built a home and studio. This was an ideal location for a budding landscape painter. I loved this great open country of mountains and forests, lakes and streams, ghost towns and old mines, canyons and deserts.

Then came the depression of '29. No one could buy paintings when he could scarcely buy beans. "We can live without pictures but not so well." Maudy Russell truly believed this famous quotation. We traded her our paintings for chickens, eggs, peaches, and grapes. A number of regional artists might have starved to death had it not been for Maudy Russell's love of art in her life and home.

At this time a WPA Art program commissioned me to execute two large murals in the auditorium of the Grand Junction High School. I worked for six months on this project for the magnificent sum of $30.00 a week, $1.00 an hour.

Several trips to Taos and Santa Fe, New Mexico, visiting and studying with the old-timers there, helped me to see more clearly just what it is that makes good paintings. Taos of thirty-five years ago was indeed fascinating. I was openly welcomed into the studios of Bert Phillips, Irving Couse, Oscar Berninghaus, Ernest Blumenschein, Ila McAfee, Nicolai Fechin and others. I am grateful for the help and friendship of this friendly group, always ready with the advice a young painter needs.

A Beaux Arts Club in Grand Junction held annual exhibitions for many years, sidewalk sales and an Artists Ball. Some of the leading members were

2

Archi Bliss, promoter and art connoisseur; Harold Bryant, nationally famous western painter, whose life story Al Look later did; Lee Rowell, who painted the dioramas at Mesa Verde National Park and the Chicago Field Museum; Connie Nowlan and H. Jacques, two fine landscape painters; Esther Reed, Jean Harper and others.

The historic drama and impact of the great Southwest urged me deeper and deeper into the canyonlands and the high blue mesas of Utah and Arizona and the Indian-Spanish country of New Mexico. The majesty of Grand Canyon tempted me, and I learned to appreciate Thomas Moran more than ever. Running the wild rivers, the Colorado and the San Juan, with Norman Nevills and Frank Wright, opened a new area for paintings and drawings. Exploring the "Island in the Sky" at the junction of the Green and Colorado rivers provided another primitive area for sketching and painting.

Arizona was one more step in reaching for new fields when I opened a gallery and studio in Sedona, Arizona. The nearby Navajo and Hopi reservations were filled with prehistoric ruins of ancient races and cultures waiting to be preserved in drawings and paintings. There were many trips to the deserts of Arizona and California, the Pacific Coast, and to Old Mexico.

This book began as my wish to bring you some of the thrill and excitement I feel when I find wild places to explore, new places, subjects and compositions to put down in paint on canvas. My guardian angel often sits on my shoulder and guides my hand. Sometimes I feel the little fellow isn't much of a painter, and then I think perhaps if I had listened more closely to what he said I might have done far better.

My deepest thanks and appreciation go to the many who made this book possible. Bob and Laurie MacLeod, Charlie Dye, Joe Beeler, Earl Carpenter and Bob Knudson, nationally prominent artists who show their paintings and sculpture in the Sedona gallery, all encouraged me. Joy Jordan deserves my special thanks as she floundered through my handwritten notes. For all these and many other friends I am grateful.

AL NESTLER

ARIZONA

ALPINE PEAKS TO SONORAN DESERT

ARIZONA, MY ADOPTED STATE these past ten years, has presented me a real challenge in trying to capture the striking beauty and the magnificent panorama of color flung with complete abandon across all parts of the state.

Colorado and Utah are divided by mountain ranges running north and south; Arizona is divided east and west. The northern part of the state is heavily forested in the higher elevations with ponderosa pine, spruce, and aspen, extending south to the Mogollon Rim. The land drops away sharply below this great escarpment to the Sonoran desert below. This is the land of the giant saguaro, the cholla, the bisnaga, and many other varieties of cacti. Palo verde, ironwood, and mesquite trees line the desert washes seeking every available bit of moisture in this arid land. If there has been a good supply of rain in the winter and spring, the desert in some years produces a wildflower display that truly must be seen to be believed. Photographers and artists vie with each other in capturing the beauty of these colorful displays. The palo verde with its lemon yellow masses of blooms has been a favorite subject of landscape painters who love the desert scene.

There is the colorful area known as Red Rock country and the beauty of Oak Creek, and within an hour or two of Sedona, the mountains and forests of the Flagstaff area, the many outstanding ruins at Wupatki, Tuzigoot, Walnut Canyon, and Montezuma Castle National Monuments; the great beauty of the Lake Powell area and Monument Valley; the fascinating Navajo and Hopi Indian reservations; the Grand Canyon; the horse and cattle ranches reminiscent of the early West, and the Sonoran desert with its completely different flora and fauna to the south.

To be the center of such a wide choice of subject matter makes Sedona an artist's paradise. No wonder that so many artists have their homes and studios there. The Sedona Art Center is one of the most active and progressive art groups in the entire West.

SHUNGOPAVI — *Oil*, 16 x 20 inches

Collection of Mr. and Mrs. Paul Weaver

Bordering Old Mexico in the southwestern part of Arizona is Organ Pipe Cactus National Monument. This is the only area in the United States where the organ pipe cactus is to be found. The entire area is a rich showplace of the native flora of the Sonoran desert. I have had much fun there with sketch pads and camera. The grassland and live oak country east of Nogales is very different from most of Arizona and affords the artist exciting compositions and patterns for his canvas.

Although my favorite sketching areas are usually in the wilder faraway places, our beautiful desert city of Phoenix and its sister cities of Scottsdale and Tucson have much of interest for the artist and layman alike. Fine museums, an abundance of art galleries covering every phase of the arts, and excellent art collections in the universities, all await your enjoyment.

Some of my favorite Arizona sketching areas are in the Sunset Crater and Wupatki National Monuments and in the Hopi villages on the high points of Black Mesa, particularly Old Oraibi.

Many are unaware that Old Oraibi, Hopi village in northern Arizona, has been continuously lived in longer than any other village or town in North America. For this reason and for the interesting types of construction of its older buildings, Oraibi has charm and fascination for artists, archaeologists, and photographers.

Hopi leaders have told me that the beautiful and expertly constructed stone houses and villages preserved in Wupatki National Monument, north of Flagstaff, were built by their ancestors before they moved east to the high mesas. Wupatki and the surrounding villages were built following the volcanic eruption of Sunset Crater in 1064 A.D.

After climbing the rugged trail to the top of Sunset Crater, I sat enjoying the view across the countless miles and tried to reconstruct a day in the fall of 1064 A.D. On an otherwise calm and beautiful day, without warning, the earth suddenly trembled. The ground heaved and buckled as great cracks shot out in all directions. Jets of steam, hot ashes and flying rocks burst through the earth and hurled themselves high into the sky. Huge clouds of cinders, smoke, and steam boiling and surging thousands of feet into the sky must have created an awesome sight. When night came, it must have been truly frightening. Cinders from this volcano rained down on over 800 square miles and many of the homes were buried under streams of lava and ashes. Surely those who survived must have fled.

As the molten cauldrons of lava cooled and plugged themselves, some of the people, curious as man has always been, returned to see what had happened. They discovered that the soil beneath the layer of ashes was moist. By nature and necessity farmers, they knew that the mulching action of the ground cover would produce their corn, beans, and other crops. So it was that the area surrounding the volcano supported one of the greatest land rushes of all times. It is estimated that upwards of 8,000 primitive people moved into this area. Various cultures came from north and south and blended into a new and good way of life, building, enjoying, and defending Wupatki.

OCTOBER SHADOWS – *Oil*, 24 x 30 inches

THREE GENERATIONS
Oil, 24 x 30 inches

When I saw the Arizona sycamores, I couldn't wait to draw and paint their dramatic shapes and beauty. Often growing in clusters, the variations of the white, green, and tan of the bark make them exciting to portray. Next to the high country aspen, the native western sycamore is my favorite tree.

10

FLAGSTAFF WINTER
Oil, 18 x 24 inches
Collection of the Museum of Northern Arizona

The "one-in-a-century" snowstorm of 1967 and 1968 left seven feet of snow on the level at Flagstaff, Arizona. A hardship for people, livestock, and wild game, in all other aspects the storm was spectacularly beautiful.

A painting becomes a composition of masses in simplified form with details covered by snow.

WUKOKI
Oil, 24 x 30 inches

What a fortress castle this must have been for many families in 1100 A.D.! A dynamic symmetry arrangement with the window in the upper right-hand shaded wall as the principal point of interest.

SUNSET CRATER
Pen and ink, 16 x 20 inches

Nearly a thousand years have passed since Sunset Crater "blew its top" and poured molten lava and ashes over hundreds of square miles of northern Arizona. Much of this lava appears to have cooled only yesterday. A forest of ponderosa pine now softens the harsh lines of the crater.

16

GRAND CANYON
Oil, 24 x 30 inches

18

To fully appreciate the magnificence of the Grand Canyon, one must see it not once but many times.

You must see it when long fingers of sunshine disperse the fog streamers of the morning and when deep snows blanket the rims. You must see it when storm clouds scrape their feet on the towers and minarets that rise from the depths. You must see it when long slants of rain dash themselves against its striped walls. Then too you must see it from the trails leading down through layer upon layer and into the inner gorge of dark granite, the foundation stone of the earth. And then you must see it by boat, guided by one of the famous "river rats," portaging its swift and shifting currents, and gaze in amazement at the color and reflections of its few calms. Then and only then will you begin to grasp the almost unearthly beauty of the mightiest of all gorges — the Grand Canyon.

RED ROCK COUNTRY
Oil, 8 x 10 inches
Collection of Ernestine Nestler

The red rock country of North Central Arizona is becoming known as one of the most outstanding scenic attractions to be found anywhere. The magnificent panorama of reds, oranges, buffs and violets splashed with utter abandon across the golds and greens and the occasional snows of the four seasons make the Sedona area truly inspiring and never to be forgotten.

20

These peaceful farmers must have feared aggression for most of the ruins in the Wupatki area indicate their defensive position. Strategically located on a point of cliff or perched on a butte, some of the walls have narrow loop-like windows. The two- and three-storied walls, still as straight and plumb as when laid, attest to the craftsmanship of these excellent stonemasons of long ago. With only mud as mortar, these well-preserved buildings are of variegated red and buff sandstone and, in some instances, of lava rock.

I shall never forget the thrill of my first visit to Wupatki. After sketching one of the ruins, we climbed the craggy cliffs on which the ancient structure stood. For as far as we could see, stonewalled ruins stood on every promontory, point, and defendable cliff and ridge. Bathed in brilliant buffs, pinks, and orange in the late afternoon sun with deep violet shadows and the black eyes of occasional windows and loopholes, the ruins appeared as eerie as if they were habitations from another planet. If our modern developers and subdividers had used just half the good taste in locating building sites as these ancient people had, wouldn't our suburban areas have been far more handsome?

One of the most interesting and exciting ruins for me is Wukoki. This old stone house on an elongated sandstone rock made it an impregnable fortress. It has, apparently, one entrance up a ladder in a crack in the rock; through a hole or door into one of the rooms, the ladder could be pulled up and the pueblo defended with ease. With its corner tower and massive curved wall at the north end of the rock, it remains one of the finest examples of primitive stone architecture in America.

What happened to the busy brown stonemasons? Why did they leave their beautiful homes erected by such tremendous effort? Where did they go? Students of such matters tell us that the century following 1200 A.D. was perhaps the driest ever known in our Southwest. Tree ring evidence indicates that from about 1215 A.D. there was a long drought of varying intensity, culminating in the great and terrible drought of the entire last quarter of the century.

High winds, carrying the cinder ground cover into dunes, and steadily decreasing rainfall resulted in the entire region being abandoned by 1300 A.D. Undoubtedly some of the people moved east to the higher mesas where they have been living their peaceful way these many generations.

And so it came that the ancestors of the Hopi people settled and built their villages on the sheer-walled tips of Black Mesa in northern Arizona.

Old Oraibi is on a point, high up on the cliffs of Third Mesa. It is generally conceded that the first village of the Hopis was Old Oraibi. Some sources contend that Oraibi has been continuously lived in since at least 1150 A.D.

At the turn of the century Oraibi had more than 1,000 population. Today it seems a dying community. The people have been divided again and again until only a few families remain.

Old Oraibi presents a challenge to record its ancient dwellings in drawings and paintings. It is my hope that Oraibi may be preserved as our national heritage of an ancient culture in our land.

COLORADO

HIGH COUNTRY

COLORADO — THE RIDGEPOLE STATE, land of shining mountains, highest state in the country — Colorado is all of these. There are more peaks over 13,000 feet here than in any other state, not excluding Alaska. A number of highway passes cross the great ranges above 12,000 feet, and many foot and horseback trails lead one over passes exceeding 13,000 feet. West Maroon Pass and Buckskin Pass near Aspen, Colorado are two such trails that switchback their way into above-timberline heights.

The climatic changes, the differing varieties of flora and fauna, and the magnificent views unfolding in every direction as one climbs into these Alpine elevations is worth every tired muscle acquired. Sketches and paintings of this country are not ordinary. Many of the storm-battered trees crawl along the ground; if they dare to reach upward, they appear as scarecrows with tattered arms stretching away from the prevailing winds and storms.

Spring comes late and fall, early in the high country. The spring buttercups literally push through the winter snowbanks in late June and July to blossom, mature, and go to seed before the September storms arrive. The lingering snowfields and glaciers among the peaks of the Continental Divide melt slowly throughout the spring and far into the summer to keep the clear streams flowing constantly.

Leadville, Aspen, Ouray, and Silverton were famous mining towns in the days of Colorado's gold and silver booms. Still remaining are many of the old mines, mills, and ghost towns with endless subjects for the artist and the photographer.

The canyons of the Gunnison and Colorado Rivers, which have their sources in the high peaks, thread their way across the western half of the state into Utah where, combined with the Green and the San Juan, they have carved the greatest canyon of them all, the Grand Canyon of the Colorado.

Then there is that great and completely different eastern area of Colorado, the high plains. This area is most interesting from an historical standpoint as it was here that the covered wagon trains of miners,

THE GOLDEN YEARS — *Oil*, 24 x 36 inches
Collection of Marcus Lawrence Memorial Hospital

settlers, buffalo hunters, and adventurers crawled westward and where they had their first view of the snowy ranges ahead. Traveling sometimes only six to ten miles a day, the mighty barrier of the Colorado Rockies must have been their morning view for many days, often no doubt seeming equally as far away as on the day before. Marauding bands of Cheyennes, Arapaho, and Comanches were a constant threat to life and peaceful progress westward.

Over the Santa Fe Trail from Independence, Missouri came the freight wagons west into Colorado to Bents Fort near the junction of the Purgatory and the Arkansas Rivers and on south to Taos and Santa Fe, New Mexico. They hauled everything necessary to life from flour to gunpowder and from farm implements to whiskey.

All of this historical drama has been the subject of countless paintings, drawings, and sculpture by some of our greatest artists. No subject is as popular in today's art market as the so-called "Westerns" portraying the lives and adventures of those who settled and built the West. To name them all is not the purpose of this book; others have already done so. The many Western painters today, following in the footsteps, or perhaps better stated, the "brush-strokes," of the Russells and Remingtons and others, are filling a nostalgic need of the art buyers and connoisseurs of today.

ASPEN — *Oil*, 24 x 30 inches

Collection of Mmes. Donna Baker and Elizabeth Hall

DESERTED HOMESTEAD
Oil, 20 x 24 inches
Collection of Mr. and Mrs. Pete King

Memories of someone's home long ago, near Durango, in southern Colorado.

If this deserted homestead could only talk, what stories it might tell us of laughter and tears, hard work and play, of the days when it was new and switches of cottonwood were planted for shade, of playing children and a barking dog. It is deserted now. The cottonwoods are bleached and stark; the weathered pine boards, rust and gray. Golden grass and sunflower stalks crowd the doorways.

LITTLE ADOBE
Watercolor, 10 x 14 inches

Near my studio in Grand Junction, this little adobe was being built for an artist. The vigas supporting the roof stuck out on the fireplace side. The protruding poles over the entrance were later covered with planks and roofing to provide shelter for the entry. Covered with adobe colored stucco, the artist's sunny studio was warm in winter and cool in summer.

30

WILLOW LAKE
Oil, 24 x 32 inches
Collection of Grand Junction Public Library

This beautiful high mountain lake is in the Aspen-Maroon Bells primitive area and is among the best of the many fine fishing lakes of the state. It lies at the last limit of tree growth and only a very few stunted trees are found on its shores. Willow Lake, probably named for the willows bordering the stream below, is reached only by horseback or afoot over a nine-mile trail from the nearest road. The study for this painting was sketched on the Fourth of July with the spring buttercups literally bursting through the snowbanks.

32

WINTER HIGHLANDS
Oil, 24 x 32 inches
Collection of U.S. Bank of Grand Junction, Colorado

This painting is of the timberline area on Red Mountain Pass near Ouray. The runoff from these high mountain snows ultimately reaches the Gunnison and Colorado Rivers and finally Lake Powell and Lake Mead, affording power, boating, and recreation for many. The S form of composition here and the dynamic symmetry arrangement will be obvious to composition "buffs."

YANKEE GIRL
Oil, 20 x 24 inches
Collection of Byron Wilson

During the 30's this silver mine near Red Mountain Pass between Ouray and Silverton was the subject for many paintings and drawings. In its heyday the Yankee Girl produced many millions for its owners. Now abandoned and falling into ruin, its dark timbered interior must know the ghosts of yesteryear.

36

MAROON PEAKS
Oil, 24 x 32 inches
Collection of Byron Wilson

38

When the last lingering rays of a setting sun cast brilliant orange and pink lights on the snow-patched peaks of the Colorado Rocky Mountains, these are exciting moments for me. The brilliantly lighted snowfields of the Maroon Bells are reflected in the placid waters of Maroon Lake near Aspen.

MT. WILSON
Oil, 24 x 32 inches
Collection of Clint Biggs

Looking through aspen trees in the spring across the snow bowl of 14,000 foot Mt. Wilson near Telluride, Colorado is a real "thriller" for artists and photographers alike. The glittering snow patches in sun and in shadow are most exciting to capture in paint. Early afternoon cumulus is billowing up and could forecast showers later in the day.

This is a simple dynamic symmetry arrangement in composition.

Moran, Bierstadt, and other great landscape painters also portrayed Colorado in their day. I recall particularly Thomas Moran's well-known "Mount of the Holy Cross." This beautiful peak lies within Holy Cross National Forest and has been a shrine for thousands throughout the years. While I was still living in Colorado, *Time* published a story of the cross on the face of the peak which told of the arm's falling away and the cross being no longer visible. This was hard for me to believe as I had seen no change in it the previous summer when I had been painting in that area. The following July, I drove to the area and hiked up the five-mile trail to Tigiwon Mountain, and there, beautiful in the late morning sun was the great cross as perfect and unspoiled as ever. I sent two photographs and slides along with dates to *Time* and received a letter of apology for its error.

The magnificent northern mountain area, most of which is included in Rocky Mountain National Park, is surely a paradise for the artist. Longs Peak and Mount Meeker, with glacial lakes nestling at the base of tremendous cliffs and crags, form some majestic compositions. Strong diagonals of ridges and talus slopes, storm-battered timberline trees and snow fields in sun and shadow are real "meat" for the painter of the mountain country. Beautiful lakes and streams abound in the area, also noted for its forests and the many varieties of wildflowers which splash their rainbow colors across the slopes and meadows.

Heavy snows make Trail Ridge Road, several miles of which are above timberline, inaccessible until June. A trip over this road to Grand Lake affords spectacular subject matter for the artist. In this same neighborhood there are springs and a tiny stream just under Lulu Pass which forms the extreme headwaters of our great western river, the Colorado. I once did a series of drawings and paintings titled "Sketching and Painting Along a Mighty River," which began at Lulu Pass and ended at the mouth of that canyon-carving river where it pours its waters into the Gulf of California.

This mountain state is indeed a challenge to any artist who tries to catch its many moods on canvas. We try and fail and try again. What fun to have tried!

UTAH

ROCK SCULPTURES: WILD RIVERS

UTAH HAS MUCH to interest artists and photographers. Imagine a sprawling many-fingered island 6,000 feet high perched atop sheer sandstone cliffs more than 2,000 feet above the mighty Colorado River on one side and the looping turbulent Green River on the other. On this island are hundreds of viewpoints overlooking a vast sea of towering buttes, spires, mesas, canyons, and distant mountain ranges in three states filling the vast purple distance in every direction.

This "Island in the Sky" in southeastern Utah is high above the triangle where the Green and Colorado rivers join forces to form the wildest, most cutting river on the face of the earth. Happily, one can drive to this sky island by car across a 30-foot roadway called The Neck.

Now mark well, whether you come by car, horseback or afoot, this extremely narrow neck is the only approach to this island mesa whose cliff-edge "shoreline" is hundreds of feet above the rockstrewn talus slopes below. Through all the blue and purple

haze and the jumble of towers, buttes, island mesas, and immense cliffs, the Colorado cuts its way deeper and deeper into the rock layers of the ages.

The snow-spattered La Sal Mountains push their sharp peaks into the eastern horizon. To the southeast are the Blue Mountains behind Monticello. Great piles of cumulus boil over and around them with slanting streaks of rain pouring from their dark bottoms to foretell showers. On the western side of the Blues, between the mountains and the Colorado River, is the famous Needles Area, a wild rugged section. Far to the south is Navajo Mountain on the Arizona border. This landmark mountain, sacred to the Navajos, piles its dome-shaped head above Rainbow Bridge.

And then there is Monument Valley — the Mittens, the Totem Pole, Rabbit Ears, and many others — magnificent rock formations sculptured by time into cathedral towers, spires, and minarets of awe-inspiring form. Until you get out of your car and walk to the base of one of these formations, you

RIVER CANYON – *Oil*, 18 x 24 inches

Collection of Mike Nelson and courtesy of Walter Foster

won't believe that many are as tall and as wide as city skyscrapers.

Monument Valley with its headlands, mesa points, buttressed walls, overhanging cliffs, shifting dunes, wind-eroded arches, natural bridges, and ancient ruins of early dwellers, is truly exalting. And the colorful Navajos still live there, herding their flocks of sheep much as they did many years ago.

Utah is mountainous, not as much so as Colorado but some of the ranges are spectacular. Such a one is the beautiful Wasatch Range which stretches some 200 miles north and south through the middle of the state. This range forms a snowy rampart on the east side of the Great Salt Lake Valley. Artists for many years have painted the beauty of these mountains often as a backdrop for the farms, orchards, old barns, and homes of this Mormon region.

The people of Utah have always been active in sponsoring music and the arts. The little city of Springville at the foot of the Wasatch is prominent in this respect and is known as the Art City of Utah. The Springville Art Association has for many years held a National Invitational Exhibition during the month of April which has attracted many of the nation's best-known painters and sculptors. These annual shows are held in an attractive two-story Arts Center with many well-lighted exhibition rooms. Through the years a permanent collection has been purchased with funds raised by the community. Valuable additions by private collectors have been donated until today the collection is rated among the best of the entire West.

The building of Glen Canyon Dam and Lake Powell has opened the southern part of Utah to boating enthusiasts and those seeking recreation in a vast wilderness area which, prior to the construction, was probably the largest truly wild area in our country.

Several years before the Glen Canyon Dam was built, I was instrumental in getting together a group of ten artist friends for a two-week trip down the San Juan and Colorado rivers. Our main effort was to photograph, sketch, and paint and to explore the many interesting side canyons of what was then regarded as some of the wildest river country in the world.

Frank Wright of Blanding was the leader of our expedition, one of the finest outdoorsmen I have ever met — quiet and unassuming, always calm, a tower of strength, and skillful with a boat in the roaring rockstrewn cataracts of these rivers.

The shore at Mexican Hat was piled high with seemingly tons of sketchboxes, easels, bedrolls, supplies, and equipment. A couple of hours later all this was neatly and deftly stowed aboard. We noted that all canned foods had the name of the contents painted on the top with waterproof paint, and by the second day we discovered why. All the labels were soaked off from repeated drenchings in the rapids and by the waves that broke over the boats.

The heavy snows near the headwaters and the rapid spring thaw had made the river at its highest stage in many years. This, according to the river men, would make excellent boating. The cataracts would be wild but the rocks, more cushioned. In minutes we had left the sunshine and plunged into

COTTONWOOD WASH — *Oil*, 18 x 24 inches

DESERT WALLS
Oil, 24 x 30 inches
Courtesy of Walter Foster

These sometimes barren but highly colored subjects, with dry sandy washes and eroded rocks, are most inspiring.

MYSTERY CANYON
Watercolor, 16 x 20 inches

50

A twisting narrow sheer-walled canyon. A small but delightful stream flowing into the Colorado. The great river at high stage had backed up almost a mile into waters where we could row our boats through a considerable portion of the canyon before beaching there. A small but well-preserved ruin was our reward for a hike upstream.

the dark, almost gloomy, gorges of the Goosenecks of the San Juan. Here the river looped and twisted in several great curves, miles in circumference, returning to within a stone's throw of itself.

The drama and rapid change of scenery carried a terrific impact. Sheer and overhanging walls rose hundreds of feet into the blue with towering spires, shafts, and minarets of every shape and size. Here was a gorge so narrow it almost seemed that by stretching a little the walls on either side might be touched with the oars. Farther on the canyon widened with beautiful white sandy beaches at the foot of flower-filled and shrubbery-spangled talus slopes.

And then we heard it. A dull rumble like distant thunder came on a downstream breeze. Louder now and more constant as we rode the current around the outside bend of a curving wall. "Government Rapid," said our boatman, "first of the majors." Our hearts crept into our throats as the downstream din grew in proportion to our forward speed. Rock piles, tiered slopes and seamed and turreted walls sped past like telephone poles from an express train. Then we saw Frank a hundred yards ahead pulling to the left bank for a landing. With sighs of relief we realized a stop was being made to look things over.

Government Rapid was our first sight of roaring, smashing, ear-splitting water churning its way through a jumbled mass of rocks, with huge waves six to ten feet high being hurled up against the rugged far wall.

The boats used by these river runners are maneuverable, and a skilled boatman literally "reads the river" as you or I would read a printed page. He

studies it carefully to see what information the boils, the holes, the choppy areas, the high waves, and the long tongues will impart to him. Our three boatmen spent nearly half an hour studying the rapids and determining the course to follow. Our boats were run through all the rapids, usually with one passenger riding along for the thrill; however, equipment and supplies, except the heavy canned goods on the bottom of the boats, were portaged around to the lower end of the rapid. Fortunately all of the six major rapids on the San Juan can be portaged.

At six o'clock Frank pulled in on a sandy beach where we made camp for the night, with driftwood for the cooking fires, flat rocks for the tables, and dry red sand on which to roll out the sleeping bags. Delicious steaks grilled over the coals were the main dish for this, our first dinner out. Everyone was tired, and even though it was the first time sleeping "out" for some, all reported next morning that they had slept like logs.

We were up at dawn, and Frank and his helpers had the cooking fire going and breakfast well under way. The smell of woodsmoke, bacon and coffee drifting along the beach made the late dawdlers hurry for chow. By seven o'clock we were on the river wondering what the new day would bring.

The variety of colors of the sandstone formations was simply beyond description. Buffs, oranges, reds, purples, browns, grays, and greens create a palette against the almost violet-blue sky which delighted and at the same time utterly dismayed this group of artists.

Then that roar again, like muffled drums. We

CANYONLANDS
Watercolor, 15 x 22 inches

54

The early morning light is especially beautiful. I have painted and photographed through the changing seasons, in summer calm and in sweeping thunderstorms. It is never the same, always fascinatingly new.

MOAB VALLEY
Oil, 24 x 30 inches

    In this peaceful valley in eastern Utah, the Colorado River finds a break in the high sandstone walls where a few miles downstream it is chewed to bits in wild, roaring Cataract Canyon.

    This painting was chosen as a Grand National Finalist from Colorado for the American Artists Professional League National Exhibit in New York in 1954.

56

could recognize it now. "Sincline Rapid," said our boatman, "and it sure is a beaut!" We landed above, climbed a talus slope to have a grandstand view of the entire rapid. I was the passenger this time as Frank shoved off. To crouch down on one's heels in the prow and see a major San Juan rapid staring you in the face takes something I wasn't quite sure I possessed. I had confidence in Frank, indeed, but when the tremendous pull of the rapid took hold of the boat and a cross-river slick seemed to be carrying us straight into the huge waves, I know my heart was choking me, but at the proper instant Frank brought her around, skirting a great hole fully ten feet deep and skimming the length of another tongue with huge protruding rocks on either side. I caught a glimpse of Ray Eggerstad on the shore getting all of this "fun" on film. Seconds later, flying through a mass of spray and foam, we curved to the left on a ripping cross current and into the clear. Wow! I shall never forget that ride.

Reaching the junction where the San Juan pours its yellow torrent into the mighty Colorado, we camped for the night near Hidden Passage and from this point we traveled much more leisurely, stopping only for drawing, sketching, and photographing. We explored Mystery Canyon, Red Bud Canyon, Music Temple, and many others. We spent two days at Nonnezoshi, the great Rainbow Bridge, one of the grandest and most magnificent spectacles in this country. As we ate our lunch near the Bridge our color-conscious group noted every color in the chart. Little wonder the Indians have a legend that the huge arch is a rainbow turned to stone.

Literally hundred of drawings and sketches came from this exciting trip into the wilds of Utah's river canyons.

NEW MEXICO

ENCHANTED LAND

ONE OF THE MOST INTERESTING FEATURES of New Mexico for artists and laymen is its large Indian population and their villages. The Pueblo Indians are scattered in a series of villages from Taos in the north to Zuni and Acoma in the western area. Others along the Rio Grande River, or near it, include the pueblos of Picuris, San Juan, Santa Clara, Nambe, San Ildefonso, Tesuque, Santo Domingo, Jemez, Zia, Santa Ana, San Felipe, Isleta, and Laguna. These stone and adobe villages with their many variations of exciting architecture and the colorful Indians themselves have been the subjects of artists, photographers, and writers almost since the time of their discovery.

After conquering the Aztecs in Mexico and the Incas in Peru and looting those tribes of much gold and other wealth, the Spanish explorers and men-at-arms heard rumors of villages with walls of turquoise and gold to the north. In February 1540, Coronado led an army of 300 men with hundreds of Indians as burden bearers into this fabled area to find gold and wealth and to take possession of the land in the name of the King of Spain. With the soldiers went the Franciscan Padres, unarmed, frocked, and sandaled, whose sole purpose was to bring the Cross and Christianity to the natives. Coronado and his men fought their first battle against the Pueblo people at what is now the Zuni Pueblo. The superior arms of the Spanish soon conquered the Pueblo but Coronado was wounded.

While recuperating at Zuni, Coronado sent Diaz, an aide, and a small party to explore westward. This party reached the junction of the Gila and Colorado rivers where they found a cross and buried letters left by Alarcon, Spanish Naval captain, who had sailed up the Colorado to the present site of Yuma, Arizona. Coronado also sent Captain Alvarado with a company of men to explore the land to the east. They passed the sky village of Acoma and continued east to Isleta Pueblo. It was near Isleta that this party became the first white explorers to see the Rio Grande Valley. Following the river north

MISSION WOODPILE – *Oil*, 20 x 30 inches
Collection of John Pflueger

they visited all of the pueblos, even crossing the sagebrush plains to Taos. This intrepid party continued on to the great plains where they saw immense herds of "cattle," the buffalo.

The following spring Coronado himself pushed eastward across what is now the Texas Panhandle and continued as far as present day mid-Kansas. At the same time DeSoto had sailed up the Mississippi. These two Spaniards had spanned the continent in 1541, and Spain laid claim to one-third of the present United States.

It was not until 1598 that further substantial exploration and colonization were attempted. General Onate with a company of 400 men, 130 with wives and children, a herd of animals to supply meat, many Indian bearers and carretas loaded with supplies of every description, crossed the Rio Grande River near El Paso and slowly struggled northward, visiting most of the Pueblos. Finally in July 1598 General Onate chose for his capital the Pueblo of San Juan within sight of the Taos Mountains and the beautiful Sangre de Christos. The Spaniards brought much that was useful to the Indians: seeds, fruit, sheep, cattle, and horses. The Padres taught their religion as well as many arts and crafts and moved forward into the 17th century with their programs of mission building. Onate was replaced as Governor by Don Pedro de Peralta, who in 1610 removed the capital and the seat of government to Santa Fe where it has remained for some 350 years.

The next 100 years and continuing into the 18th century saw most of the mission churches of the entire Southwest constructed. These beautiful structures have been the subjects of much interest. Artists, architects, pilgrims, and tourists have been thrilled with the native constructed, handcrafted appearance of both exteriors and interiors of these missions. This architecture has become known as Pueblo Spanish style. Walls of adobe bricks or stone are often four to six feet thick with massive timbers supporting the pole and dirt roofs.

After three-quarters of a century of colonizing New Mexico and building many missions, a severe drought plagued the colonists and Indians. Warlike Apaches brought trouble, and the missions and pueblos east of the Monzano Mountains were abandoned. The ruins of these magnificent structures are included today in the Gran Quivira National Monument.

There was much unrest among the pueblos, fanned by certain medicine men, notably one, Pope of San Juan. This hatred against the Spanish overlords culminated in the rebellion of 1680 when many of the priests were killed and most of the missions were burned and destroyed. Governor Otermin and the Spanish people not killed in the rebellion were forced to flee south to Mexico. This abandonment of Spain's northern colony was the worst setback that powerful empire had ever known.

New Mexico was Indian again and much of beauty and good had been destroyed. In 1692 Don Diego de Vargas marched north to reconquer the lost province. The conquest was fairly peaceful as many Indians no doubt felt that the Spanish with their superior weaponry could protect them from the warlike enemies to the north and east. However,

TAOS PUEBLO — *Oil*, 12 x 16 inches   Courtesy of Walter Foster

HIGH FALL
Oil, 18 x 24 inches
Collection of Mr. and Mrs. Martin Nestler

This old weathered barn in New Mexico has been the subject of numerous drawings and paintings. The gray-with-age boards of roof and fence lend themselves beautifully as subject matter for the artist. This was especially true in the fall when some old cottonwoods were burnished gold in the sun.

MISSION AT ACOMA
Felt pen, 11 x 14 inches

The Sky Village of Acoma is famous for the Mission of Saint Stephen established in 1629 by a Franciscan Brother, Juan Ramirez. Built largely of adobe bricks, the constant wind and water erosion of the centuries has made this largest of the early mission churches difficult to keep in good repair. From high scaffolding, the Acomas are now facing the ancient walls with a thick layer of native rock — truly a labor of many stones.

EARLY MORNING TAOS
Oil, 18 x 24 inches
Collection of Dr. S. L. Biggs

68

The blanketed Taos women carry themselves with grace as they walk in the plaza and lanes of their village and climb the ladders to the upper stories of their pueblo.

Nectler =0=

many minor skirmishes and battles with Indian holdouts took place and it was not until 1696 that the reconquest was over and colonists and settlers again could live in peace.

One of the finest examples of the early Franciscan missions and one of the few to escape destruction during the Pueblo Rebellion, is the beautiful mission at Zia Pueblo. The white stuccoed façade consists of a balcony and a portico flanked on either side by thick end walls. The walled Compo Sonto or church yard is the burial place of many Zia villagers. On her festival day, August 15, the small image of the Virgin of the Assumption is taken from her special place on the altar and carried about the village in an impressive ceremonial. The mission houses a fine painting of the Assumption given by a Spanish family in 1798. Zia is one of the oldest of the pueblos and was visited by Coronado, Espejo, Onate, and de Vargas.

The great mission at Acoma, established in 1629, is a monument of human endeavor. It is more than 150 feet long and 40 feet wide. On either side are huge sloping buttresses topped by square towers. Adjoining are the conventos and a lookout tower from which in early days approaching enemies might be sighted. The curved vigas, one foot square and over forty feet long, support the roof. These timbers were carried by the Indians from a mountain area many miles distant, then up the tortuous trail to the summit of the rock. A quaint altar and many Santos and paintings grace the interior. A painting of St. Joseph presented by the King of Spain is a most prized possession. It was credited with bringing prosperity to the village, and to better their own poor circumstances the neighboring village of Laguna took the painting. They too began to prosper and refused to return it. The matter was finally taken to court which returned the painting to the rightful owners at Acoma.

The village of Acoma today, high on its rocky island mesa, is known as the Sky Village. Although some of its people have moved into areas near their employment, many still live in this old village. I found them friendly and proud of their heritage. Their dwelling places of two or three stories required ladders to reach the upper heights. The ancient builders were the first in America to design the stepped-back architecture we know today in our high rise buildings. Huge timber vigas support the heavy mud-and-pole roofs.

The light and shadow patterns against the stone and adobe walls, the ancient doorways and the overhanging portals are irresistible from an artist's viewpoint, all forming exciting compositions. Many drawings and paintings have been the result of visits to this beautiful island mesa and its village, the home of some of our earliest Americans.

Truchas and Trampas, settled by families who found Santa Fe too crowded in the 1700s, delight the eye. Century-old barns of heavy timbers and handsawn planks, strawstacks, privies — all fill my sketchbooks. There are many other objects of beauty — the Penitente crosses, a mission woodpile, a rocky mesa.

CALIFORNIA

LAND OF CONTRAST

CALIFORNIA IS MOST INTERESTING historically for here, as in New Mexico, the Spanish explorers in the 1700's established many missions and settlements — from San Diego in the south to Santa Barbara and Monterey and San Francisco in the north. Land grants by the King of Spain to prominent Spanish families, soon built up a cattle and livestock industry presided over by the Spanish vaquero, the buckaroo of California.

In 1858 the famous Butterfield Stage lines from St. Louis to San Francisco, entering California at Yuma, brought many notable people — investors, engineers, miners and promoters — all seeking footholds in a new land. At its peak this stage line required 1800 horses and mules, 250 coaches, many freight and water wagons, and some 2000 employees. At the outbreak of the Civil War the route was changed to cross the central part of the country. Wells Fargo and Company took over the line later and both finally gave way to the coming of the transcontinental trains. Some of the old stage sta-

tions are still in existence and have been the subjects of paintings and drawings by many artists.

The Pony Express also brought the mails from St. Joseph, Missouri to Sacramento about this time, making the 1,960 mile trip by single riders in ten days.

The Joshua Tree National Monument, with its forest of unusual trees and its mountains of weathered granite rock piles, has furnished much subject matter for artists, camera fans, and writers.

California has much natural beauty, far more perhaps than most states, but as everywhere else, much of it is in danger of being lost in these days of commercialization and destruction by selfish interests. May we salute the conservation groups, historical societies, and anti-pollution groups fighting to keep this great state truly great.

Artists who live in California are indeed fortunate, for they can spend a lifetime and never exhaust their subject matter — from the highest point on Mt. Whitney to the lowest in Death Valley, from

DUNE PATTERNS — *Oil,* 30 x 24 inches

the arid deserts in the south to the rain forests in the north, and from the ocean to the Sierras.

When I first visited the groves of redwoods and sequoias, I was filled with amazement and then awe for the grandeur of these mighty trees. Walking through their forests is like walking into a cathedral. In morning fog one thinks of stained glass windows and marble pillars. Shafts of sunlight filter through the branches. How does one paint these trees? I have yet to attempt it.

There are rocky coves and beautiful beaches. Marine paintings in great quality and quantity have been done by artists of the West Coast.

The old missions of early Spanish days have produced a wealth of murals and paintings done by a stream of creative and imaginative artists of yesteryear.

Before the days of barbed wire, the early settlers constructed miles upon miles of redwood fences, a few of which still remain. They form beautiful patterns as they climb and wind over the rolling slopes and fields along the coastline.

There are many kinds of trees, from the tallest on earth to the palms in the canyons and the humble smoke trees of the desert washes. The little smoke tree is a chameleon. Against shaded canyon walls it seems pale green; against a sunny sky or sandy wash, blue gray and orange; in full bloom, deep blue violet, as it is covered with blossoms like small sweet peas.

SMOKE TREE — *Oil*, 16 x 20 inches
Collection of Mr. and Mrs. T. A. Magee

PATH TO THE SEA
Oil, 24 x 30 inches
Collection of Mr. and Mrs. William (Dutch) Seebold

A pathway to the beach. A split rail fence with its shadow cast by an afternoon sun.

76

GATEWAY TO YESTERDAY
Watercolor, 22 x 30 inches

Like a gateway to yesterday, this scene spoke to me clearly, "Preserve me in a painting before I depart."

SAILS OF OLD
Watercolor, 15 x 20 inches

Most artists enjoy a change of pace at times with a greater variety of subject matter. This old sailing vessel of long ago, now serving as a museum near San Diego, was a dockside study in reflections and light and shadow patterns which I found most interesting.

80

OLD MEXICO

RECUERDOS OF OLD MEXICO

THROUGH CUSTOMS AT NOGALES. 10:00 A.M. Bright sunny day. *Guaymas.* Bougainvillaea and Cup of Gold blooming at our door. Fishermen unloading. Red and magenta and chartreuse sunset across the harbor. Heard often during day, "Ay que perrito" — our French poodle. *Ciudad Obregon.* Cashed $100 check American and got 1,249 pesos. Felt rich. Papaya orchards — fine eating too. *Culiacan.* Fra Marcos de Niza and Coronado passed here in 1540. A primitive village of thatched huts and open brick cooking fires. Bought pop for twenty-eight kids. Schoolteacher comes twice a month for one day. Many sketches of homes. Carretas. *Mazatlan.* Fine tile work and mosaics. Brick yards. Handmolded adobe, fired in woodburning kilns. *San Blas.* Former Spanish Consulate built in 1560, now hotel. Jungle river by boat: tropical birds, banana and coffee plantations, orchids, half-wild pigs, mangrove thickets. Parrot at hotel just couldn't "dig" Popcorn, the poodle. *Tepic,* capital of Nayarit. Army post: bugle and marching men at 5:00 A.M. Huge volcanoes, lava flows, pines and ash trees, very mountainous. Some good sketches. Maguey plants, row upon row. Tequila and pulque. *Guadalajara.* White-gloved traffic cops. Huge new market, acres of shops selling everything under the sun. Autos, donkey carts, goods-laden pedestrians, bicycles in a maddening rush of traffic. Two haystacks going down road supported by tiny donkeys. Old gray haired man kneeling before a cross at side of road. Round, pole-and-plastered corn cribs on stilts. Long file of white goats. Charcoal plant. Burro-laden vendors carrying charcoal for cooking fires. *Tlaquepaque,* village of artisans, pottery makers, glass blowers. Mexican furniture. Copper and brass inlaid with malachite. Mosaics, wrought iron, lamps, colorful weaving, woolen jackets and serapes. Orozco's home and studio — some fine works remaining. Pregnant mother with baby slung in shawl on her back followed by two toddlers. Burro trains of firewood. Man unloading metates at market. Large herd of vari-colored goats crossing road driven by serape-clad boy with

84

CALLE EN PATZCUARO — *Oil*, 24 x 30 inches

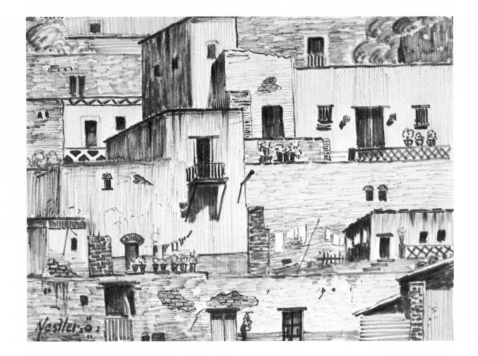

pole. Two women walking up steep trail with huge baskets on their heads. Man with team of oxen plowing hillside. *Lake Chapala*, largest in Mexico, clogged with water lilies which float with the wind. Many "Yanquis" live here. Weavers, looms, and lovely fabrics. White serapes. Fisherman of Lake Chapala. Over high mountains. Rain. Rain. Rain. Posada de Don Vasco. *Lake Patzcuaro*. Fruit cup, soup, white fish and sauce, rice with tiny dried fish, sausage, cabbage, squash, salad, frijoles, pastry, and coffee — 25 pesos. Butterfly fishermen, dugout canoes, Tarascan Indians. The island Janitizio, maguey fiber rugs. Sketched all day in the village, many beautiful subjects. Over two high passes to 10,000 feet, pines and spruce like Colorado. Four-lane highway and so to *Mexico City* and the Paseo de la Reforma. Traffic maddening. Excavations under a building bringing up piles of skulls and bones. Aztec? Christmas Eve. Service at Church of the Good Shepherd. Chapultepec. Jenas. The mosaics at the University, murals, bullfight, toreadors, picadors, cruel and bloody. *Teotihuacan* and the temple of Quetzalcoatl, sculpture and stone carvings. 16th century churches. *Taxco*, Colonial Mexico, steep hillsides, cobbled streets, silver mines, jewelry makers and craftsmen. My guide, Angel, a blue-eyed ten-year-old. Wonderful studies for paintings and camera. Marimba band, balcony and bougain-

PESCADORES DE CHAPALA — *Oil,* 24 x 30 inches
Collection of Dr. and Mrs. John Stilley

EVER SO HUMBLE
Oil, 16 x 20 inches

This little adobe house at Alamos with its tall pole fence and grass-grown dirt roof was a challenge from the moment I saw it. Waiting for better lighting, I painted it when a bright winter sun warmed its lowliness and gave strength to the shaded areas.

EL LENADOR
Oil, 24 x 30 inches

90

I was doing a drawing of the adobe buildings in this picture when this blue-trousered Mexican with his burros loaded with firewood literally walked into the scene. The moment he did, I knew that he and his burros belonged there. This village is near Guanajuato in the far south. A simple dynamic symmetry arrangement in composition.

villea. The market at Cuernavaca. Indian women with wide space between great toe and the next from lifelong wearing of toe-strap sandals, cooking food over tiny charcoal stoves on sidewalk, smells delicious. People going to market loaded down. People leaving market loaded with purchases. *Puebla and Cuautla.* Fine views of Popocatepetl and Ixtacihuatl, among Mexico's highest. Popocatepetl, ancient volcano, still spurts steam and smoke, covered far down its slopes with glacial ice and snow. Small boy, six, with great load of wood size of bushel basket on back and machete in hand. Small brother, three, with armload of sticks. Worn huaraches and dirty feet. Tile-roofed adobe hut with huge bougainvillea over fence and roof. Coca-Cola, Pepsi Cola, Orange Crush — their trucks everywhere. The national drink? Miles and miles of maguey-sisal drying on racks at twine and rope factories. Sugarcane fields and winding mountain roads to *Oaxaca.* Magnificent churches, old and new, from ancient ruins of early day monasteries and churches to new modern structures. Church bells ringing. The amazing ruins of Monte Alban, Mitla and Yagul, ancient races and cultures. Much subject matter to draw and paint. Fences of growing cactus. Roosters crowing at 4:00 A.M. A barefoot peddler selling black obsidian arrowheads dug from a ruin. Upon close questioning he grins and admits he made them himself. A glassy-eyed drunk supported by a friend. Carretas with huge loads drawn by oxen. Turkey vultures tearing flesh from a horse dead at the side of the road. A beautiful flower garden at the side of a palm-thatched hut. Hay stored in giant many-armed cactus above the reach of cows and burros. A baby burro, not much larger than a jackrabbit, with its mother. *Guanajuato.* Early silver mines, narrow streets and lanes, beautiful stone arch bridges. Many sketches. Artist could spend months, years, here. *Zimapan.* Posada del Rey. High in mountains. Fine decorations, paneling, carvings, paintings, Taberna des Liones, wine casks. Rain, fog, down to tropics again. Bananas, pineapples, coffee berries spread to dry. Houses of bamboo with sugarcane thatched roofs. Gulf of Mexico.

A picturesque and exciting country, from coast to coast, from highest mountain peaks to palm-lined tropical shores, from ancient civilizations to burgeoning new communities and modern architecture. Mexico is a continuous *fiesta* for artists.